Leslyn in London

Leslyn in London

Grace Nichols

Illustrated by Annabel Large

HODDER AND STOUGHTON

LONDON   SYDNEY   AUCKLAND   TORONTO

To Lesley

British Library Cataloguing in Publication Data

Nichols, Grace
  Leslyn in London.
  I. Title
  823[J]   PZ7

  ISBN 0–340–34954–9

Published by Hodder and Stoughton Children's Books,
a division of Hodder and Stoughton Ltd, Mill Road,
Dunton Green, Sevenoaks, Kent TN13 2YJ

Photoset by Rowland Phototypesetting Ltd
Printed and bound in Great Britain by T. J. Press (Padstow) Ltd

Contents

CHAPTER I

This is the Place, Man?

'I don't know what will become of that child,' said Grandma, wiping away a tear from her cheek as she watched the taxi taking Leslyn and her mother to the airport, drive away slowly.

Leslyn was her busybody of a grand-daughter and Leslyn was going to London to live with her father who was studying there. She and her mother, Mars, that is.

Grandma had heard all about London – what a big busy city it was and how children had to stay indoors a lot, especially in winter when it was cold. So she couldn't help feeling a bit worried to see her grand-daughter go. She had helped to care for her from the time she was a tiny baby and she knew that Leslyn wasn't a stay-indoor type of child at all.

Leslyn was accustomed to playing in the open with her cousins and friends and running on ground made warm by the sunshine. And if you did manage to get her to stay inside, she was always leaning through the open front window, watching the rumble and tumble of traffic and chatting with the people going by.

If there was one thing that Leslyn loved it was a good chat.

Their white wooden house in Georgetown, the capital of Guyana, was also near to a big market. From her front window Leslyn could see the high market clock tower and could even catch a glimpse of a few of the stalls piled up with fruits and vegetables.

Well, it was nothing like Guyana when she and her mother arrived at Heathrow Airport in London.

It was a cold smoky grey morning in late October.

Leslyn gave a gasp when she stepped from the plane and felt the icy wind going right through her, even though she was wearing a little jacket.

Clinging and shivering on her mother's arm, she looked up for a moment at the high grey buildings around her – buildings that looked as if they were growing, she thought, trying to reach the skies!

Her father was there to meet them of course with proper warm coats and scarves. He was smiling like anything when he swung Leslyn high up into his arms for a kiss. Leslyn, who hadn't seen him for the whole year, thought that just like the place he looked different too, strange with that hood pulled over his head.

A small puff of smoke came from her mouth, the way it did in winter, as she huddled into the taxi cab with her mother and father.

Her mother and father couldn't stop talking because they had so much to tell each other. Her father sat in the middle with his arms around both of them and Leslyn stared out of the window as the taxi swept along – under bridges and over bridges and past squares with tall statues. Then it kept turning off into different streets. Leslyn could see big red double-decker buses streaming along with the rest of the traffic and people walking on pavements, cloaked-up in their coats.

Before she knew it the taxi was pulling up into a street where there was hardly any sign of people or traffic around.

'This is the place, man?' Leslyn asked, when she was finally standing on the pavement. 'This is the place?'

'Yes, Miss Lady, this is the place,' said her father cheerfully, as he went around to get their things from the back of the taxi. 'Don't worry, you'll get used to the life,' he added.

Leslyn stared around her.

The street they had come to was one of those quiet back streets with two rows of brownish looking brick houses facing each other. The houses were all closed-up as if nobody lived in them and the few flowers in some of the small front gardens were withering.

Leslyn remembered the photographs her father had sent back of himself. Nice, bright, laughing photographs. She had especially liked the one of him stooping down with a pigeon perched on top of his head and hundreds more flocking around him. And the one of him with a big fountain in the background, and bright shops and people.

She couldn't see a thing like that on this street. Not even a face peeping from a window.

To make matters worse in the house where her father lived with his cousins there were no other children to play with. Only Cousin Lucille and Cousin Frank, and Cousin Lucille's old mother, Nen, who had grown accustomed to leading a quiet life.

But here she was in London.

CHAPTER 2

Sherry Come Back!

Of course Leslyn wasn't the kind of child to mope around for long, even though London wasn't quite what she had expected so far.

In no time she was visiting Nen in her bedroom and borrowing her walking stick and trying to get her to play games like, 'Which-Hand?' which was very easy. All you had to do was hide any little thing in one of your hands and ask someone else to guess which hand it was in.

Nen, wasn't always in the mood to play games, however, and especially didn't like anyone waking her up in the middle of her mid-morning nap to do so. Or borrowing her walking stick either.

But poor Leslyn hadn't anyone else to play with.

Her father had started back out to his college again. Her mother was in bed with what seemed like the flu. Cousin Lucille and Cousin Frank were at work, and Leslyn hadn't even seen any children that she could play with.

Mars managed to get up from time to time to see what Leslyn was up to.

'Don't fatigue Nen,' she pleaded each time she got up, 'find something to do like painting.'

Sometimes her mother would switch on the television for her and sometimes when Leslyn got tired of looking she pretended to be a television news reader.

She would sit up straight on the sofa with a sheet of white paper and make up her own news.

'A million people was killed today when an airplane crashed into a mountain

Five thousand milk bottles was stolen from Buckingham Palace and fifty policemen was injured

A lion was kidnapped from the zoo and twelve horses got lost in the snow . . .'

she would read on, liking the important sound of her own voice.

'Look, why you don't put on your coat and run around in the garden outside, eh,' suggested Nen, a few mornings after Leslyn's arrival in London. Leslyn had given her toy monkey a bubble bath and had left a splashy green bathroom behind.

'Go, on, do,' urged Nen, 'run around outside and let off some steam.'

Leslyn, who was only too glad to do just that, pulled on her coat quickly in case Mars decided to come downstairs and stop her. She knew that her mother wasn't quite certain about the English weather. Didn't know if it was a good thing for children to play outside in the cold or not. But Nen knew better.

The air felt like cold wet silk on Leslyn's face as she stood there, down at the small front gate, watching a car pull out from across the street, and wondering what she could do.

Leslyn remembered Nen telling her about an old man called Mr Martin who lived next door, at number 17. Leslyn was just thinking that maybe she could go round and pay him a visit when who should she see coming down the pavement, but a well dressed oldish looking lady with a small white dog on a chain.

The dog was wearing a kind of padded jacket around its middle, and Leslyn who had never seen a dog in anything but its own skin, quickly opened the gate and stepped outside.

She was afraid of big dogs because in Guyana most people kept their dogs as watch dogs and they were nearly always big and fierce and snapping.

This one was so small and was stepping along so nice and briskly that her whole face glowed with delight.

'He's your dog?' she asked as the lady got to where she was standing.

'Yes,' smiled the lady, 'but it's a she and her name's Sherry.'

'Sherry,' repeated Leslyn, staring down at the little dog as if she couldn't believe her eyes. It

didn't seem like a puppy because it had a grown-up kind of face and yet it couldn't be a grown-up dog because it was so small. Leslyn didn't know what to think.

'What she wearing around her, man?' she asked after a moment.

'That's her coat, dear,' explained the lady, 'to keep her warm.'

'She feeling cold?' asked Leslyn.

'I expect she is,' said the lady, 'just as how we feel cold I expect they feel it too.'

'How old is she?' inquired Leslyn.

'She's three years old, dear,' said the lady, beginning to move along.

And because the dog was stepping along so nice and lightly, and because it looked as if it might be a nice feeling to hold the chain, Leslyn couldn't help going after the lady and asking:

'Please let me hold her for you a little while,' and reached out to take the chain from the lady's hand.

'She likes children , dear, but she isn't accustomed to anyone else but me,' said the lady smiling, but holding on to the chain firmly all the same.

'Pleaseeeeee,' said Leslyn putting on her most pleading voice, 'please, just for a little while.'

'It isn't you, dear,' the lady tried to explain, 'it's just that she isn't accustomed to it.'

'Pleaseeeee,' said Leslyn who didn't give up easily.

'Well, just for a little while,' said the lady relenting, 'but do be very careful.'

Leslyn was very careful. She gripped the small loop attached to the chain and the dog trotted ahead of her lightly.

Just as she had expected it was a nice feeling.

The lady hurried behind her smiling anxiously. After a little while she called out, 'Come on, dear, hadn't you better be going back home now?'

Leslyn pretended that she didn't hear because she was enjoying the feeling so much. When she slackened her grip on the chain she could even feel the little dog pulling her along instead.

'Really, dear,' said the lady catching up with her.

Reluctantly, Leslyn slowed down, though the small dog was still pulling.

'Thanks for letting me hold your dog,' said Leslyn as she let go of the chain into the lady's hand.

Leslyn didn't know how it happened, but the next thing she knew, the chain fell with a rattle on to the pavement.

Both Leslyn and the oldish lady bent at the same time to pick it up almost bouncing their heads together. But just at that same time the little dog ran forward a little.

Leslyn and the lady ran forward a little too and had almost got the end of the chain when the dog darted ahead again.

'Sherry, you naughty girl. Come back here at

once,' cried the lady as she straightened up.

'Don't worry, I'll get her for you,' called out Leslyn reassuringly as she darted behind the little dog.

They were nearing the end of the street now and could see a car coming towards them.

'Sherry! Sherry! come back here,' the lady was calling shrilly now, because she was terrified that her little dog might be run over.

But the little dog didn't run across the road. She stood at the grassy corner of the street and began to sniff around, as if she had already had her bit of fun. Leslyn, who was just behind her, grabbed hold of the chain.

'A good thing you had me to help you,' she told the lady, panting a little as she handed over the chain.

But the lady didn't say anything to that. Leslyn watched them walking away for a moment. Then she ran all the way back home, thinking it was a good thing she was there to help.

CHAPTER 3

A Punch in the Belly

The very next day Leslyn's mother and father decided that it was better if Leslyn went to school after all, instead of staying home to get accustomed to the place, as they had felt in the beginning. Nen said that she thought it was the best thing too.

Leslyn's mother and father went in to see the headmistress of the junior school a few blocks away and it was the 3rd of November to be exact, when she started out to the Fendon Park Junior School.

Leslyn felt both excited and a little afraid as she walked with her parents on that very first morning. Mars had done Leslyn's hair the way she liked it, in lots of different plaits with small coloured beads that jingled whenever she moved her head.

As they came nearer to the school Leslyn could see other children coming along too, all buttoned and zipped up in their coats and anoraks. The school was near to a big park and was a big brownish building surrounded by a thick grey wall.

There was a lady wearing a kind of uniform, standing in the middle of the road with a 'Stop – Children' sign and the traffic had to wait while the children crossed over.

Leslyn's mother and father didn't wait around with the other parents in the playground outside the school. Instead they took her straight to the headmistress's office.

The headmistress, a tall, plump lady called Mrs Cox, shook Leslyn's hand and said, 'I hope you'll be very happy here with us, Leslyn. You'll be in the first year junior with Miss Sander.'

Leslyn only bit the tip of her finger as she did whenever she felt a bit nervous.

Then the children were trooping into school and her parents had to go.

Mars handed the headmistress an envelope with Leslyn's dinner money, then they kissed her goodbye. 'Don't look so worried,' she said, 'you'll be all right.'

Leslyn never felt so alone as she watched her mother and father walking away.

'Come with me, Leslyn,' said the headmistress, walking down the school corridor briskly. Leslyn followed behind and all the children coming into school stared at her.

'Here we are,' said the headmistress, turning to give Leslyn a smile as she stopped in front of a red classroom door. She pushed the door open and in they walked.

Immediately, Leslyn could feel all the eyes of the children in the room upon her. Blue eyes, black eyes, green eyes, brown eyes, all staring.

'This is Leslyn, Miss Sander,' the headmistress was saying, 'Our new girl starting today. She's from Guyana.'

Miss Sander, a young teacher in blue jeans, smiled at Leslyn and asked what her full name was when the headmistress had left.

'Leslyn Allenye,' said Leslyn, speaking suddenly quietly in the strange classroom.

'Well children,' began Miss Sander brightly, 'it is nice to have children from different countries in our class, isn't it? Maybe Leslyn will tell us something about her country when she's settled in, but right now what should you say to Leslyn?'

'Welcome to Fendon Park Junior School,' sang

the children who were all seated on small chairs around tables.

Leslyn was glad when she was seated too, at a table with five other children. But suddenly she wished she was back in her old classroom, sitting on a bench instead, with her best friend Claire pressed up close beside her.

Her new classroom was bright with pictures and drawings all around the walls. The children had their books and pencils and things tucked away in trays under some big desks.

Leslyn stared at everything in the new classroom and at the new faces around her. Back in Guyana she was used to seeing people mostly with black and brown faces. But here nearly all the children in her class were white. There was only one other brown Indian girl and another girl looking like herself.

Leslyn wondered who would be her best friend.

Just then a brown-haired boy called Jonathan leaned across the table and said, 'Gary 'ere says you're a chocolate face. Says you live in a chocolate factory, he says.'

Nobody had ever called her chocolate face before in her life.

Leslyn glared at Jonathan and the blond-haired boy she supposed was Gary. But she couldn't think of anything to say.

At break-time they all went out into the big sprawling playground to play. Most of the girls in her class ran off to play on the climbing frame.

Leslyn wandered around the playground for a while. It seemed as if there were children everywhere, running and climbing and shouting. Some of the bigger boys were playing football in one corner of the ground and Leslyn went a little closer to have a look.

'Hey-ya nig-nog,' said a biggish looking boy as he ran past her, nearly knocking her over.

Leslyn didn't know what a nig-nog was.

Then suddenly, as she stood there watching, a girl with long brown plaits came rushing up to her breathlessly.

'Would you like to come to my party?' she asked.

Leslyn could hardly believe her luck. She was too surprised to answer for a moment.

'Would you like to come to my party?' repeated the girl impatiently. Leslyn nodded.

'There'll be ice-cream and jelly and a punch in the belly and you can't watch telly 'cause your feet're too smelly,' said the girl quickly, and the next moment she was off, running.

Leslyn could only stare at her and repeat the lines to herself:

'Would you like to come to my party
There'll be icecream and jelly
and a punch in the belly
and you can't watch telly
'cause your feet're too smelly.'

CHAPTER 4

*I Want a Real Bonfire,
Not Rubbish*

At mid-day she went down with the other children into the big dinner hall where tables and
chairs were already laid out everywhere. The
dinner ladies, dressed in their white caps and
aprons, were standing behind a long counter with
the food, all ready to serve. Back in Guyana
children went home for their lunch at midday so
Leslyn had never eaten in school before.

She stood in a line with the others waiting her
turn and watching the small heaps of mashed
potatoes and mince stew and green peas that were
being put on to the plates.

'I don't want that,' she said quickly to the
dinner lady who was about to put two scoops of
mashed potatoes on her plate.

The dinner lady stared at her for a moment.
'Well you don't have to eat it ducky, leave it at the
side of your plate,' she said at last, passing the
plate to another lady who put on the mince and
peas.

'You shouldn't tell the dinner ladies what to

give you,' said a girl called Amanda in a grown-up voice as she came behind Leslyn.

Leslyn sat down at a long table with about a dozen other children and began to eat. She didn't like the mashed potatoes much. But she liked the apple crumble and custard that they had afterwards for dessert.

The children were all chattering away as they ate and they were nearly all talking about someone called Guy Fawkes and bonfires. Leslyn didn't know a thing about Guy Fawkes.

'We're having a big bonfire in our back garden, boasted Jonathan, 'and my father's buying me a lot of fireworks.'

'We're having fireworks too,' said another boy called Mick.

'And us,' said Gary.

'Do you have Guy Fawkes in Guyana, Leslyn?' inquired Amanda who was sitting beside Leslyn.

Leslyn had to admit that they hadn't. She shook her head as she finished off her custard.

'What you have in Guyana then?' demanded Jonathan.

'Mashramani,' said Leslyn as that was the only thing she could think of right then.

'Mashra-man-ee,' cried Gary, trying to mimic Leslyn's voice. 'Blimey, what's that?'

Nearly everyone at the table began to laugh. Even Bisi, the quiet little Nigerian girl whom everyone called 'Bisi-Bosi', was shaking with laughter.

Leslyn decided there and then that she wasn't going to tell them a thing about Mashramani. Not a thing.

Mashramani was a Guyanese festival, you see, and it meant 'celebration after a harvest'. It was a time when people took to the streets dressed in wonderful costumes and there was steelband dancing and floats parade. There was also a Children's Costume Competition and Leslyn had won a prize earlier in that very year when she had dressed up as a brightly feathered toucan. The Mayor had placed a shining round medal on a blue ribbon around her neck for winning one of the prizes.

But she wasn't going to tell them about that.

That afternoon her teacher spoke about Guy Fawkes in class. Leslyn listened, hanging on to every word that the teacher said, as she was the only one who didn't seem to know anything about him.

'He was the man who tried to blow up King James the first and his Parliament, years and years ago,' explained the teacher and even though he didn't succeed people still celebrated the discovery of his plot with things like bonfires and fireworks.

After the explaining, they all painted pictures about Guy Fawkes Night with big bonfires and Leslyn could think of nothing else but him for the rest of the afternoon.

She told her mother all about Guy Fawkes as they walked home from school and as soon as her father came home, before he could even catch his breath, she began to explain about it excitedly again.

'He's the man who tried to blow up King James the first and his Parlee-a-ment. But he didn't get to blow them up. But you still have to have bonfires and fireworks. Our teacher say so and all the children in the school having bonfires and fireworks . . .' she went on.

'Let me sit down and enjoy this food first,' said her father, patting her head, 'then we can talk about Guy Fawkes and fireworks.' And he pulled out his chair, sat down and took a big mouthful of his black-eye cook-up-rice.

'All the other children having bonfires . . .' Leslyn began again.

'Girl, shut up about Guy Fawkes for a little while!' said Mars. 'You're giving me a headache.'

'What's all this about bonfire?' inquired Nen who was just coming downstairs to look at her favourite Crossroads on television.

'All I begging you is not to burn me out of house and home,' she went on, 'every year some child or other always getting burnt from this Guy Fawkes nonsense.'

Leslyn burst into tears. 'You all don't want me to have anything for Guy Fawkes,' she wept.

'Look, love,' said her father, putting down his spoon, 'Guy Fawkes is an English-people custom. We don't know much about Guy Fawkes, but if it

28

will make you happy we can get rid of some rubbish tomorrow night – burn it,' he added quickly his eyes sparkling with mischief.

Leslyn was nearly in tears again. 'I want a real bonfire. Not rubbish,' she choked.

'But what you think they burn in bonfires, eh?' asked her father. 'Rubbish, old papers and things.'

'And fireworks?' asked Leslyn. 'Could we get some fireworks too?'

'I can't promise you fireworks, love,' said her father, 'but definitely we have a date with the bonfire tomorrow night.'

'Oh, all right then,' said Leslyn, finishing her tears. She supposed that was better than having nothing at all.

CHAPTER 5

It's Too Late to Burn Him Now

'We're having a bonfire,' Leslyn told the children at school the next day.

'So what?' said Gary, 'We're having a bonfire and fireworks as well.'

'Yes, so what?' smirked Jonathan, 'a bonfire by itself is nothing really.'

Leslyn was still excited by their own bonfire however, and she was glad when the school day came to an end.

Mars, was waiting for her, standing a little way off from the other mums who were laughing and talking among themselves. Leslyn couldn't help feeling a little sorry for her mother, because she suddenly looked lonely standing there all by herself. Maybe she was missing her friends too and the things she did back home, like acting in plays down at the Theatre Guild.

It didn't seem as if you could make friends easily in this country, Leslyn thought. Yesterday, when school was over for the day, all the children had hurried away with their parents into different directions. Some into cars. Others just hurrying away, out of the cold darkish afternoon.

But she soon cheered up when they got home. Her mother had made some of her favourite coconut fudge and the house was nice and warm.

Leslyn hurried into the back garden as soon as she was finished eating to have a look at the old iron crate in which they were going to have their bonfire.

Her mother had already collected some pieces of dried twigs which she had thrown at the bottom of the crate and Leslyn went on looking around to see what else she could find.

She wasn't looking for very long when suddenly she heard a sound, as if someone had knocked a milk bottle over. Looking around Leslyn saw a small old man bending at the side of his garden shed next door.

That must be Mr Martin, the old man whom Nen was telling her about.

Leslyn ran to the mesh fence at once and called out, 'Hello.'

The old man straightened up and came towards her.

He was a very small man with thin silvery hair.

'Hello,' he said in a trembly kind of voice.

'You're Mr Martin,' Leslyn told him, 'I'm Leslyn. I'm from Guyana.' You have any children to play with?' she asked hopefully, even though Nen had already told her that Mr Martin

31

lived all by himself, and that his wife had died a few years ago.

Mr Martin shook his head, 'I don't have any children here,' he said, 'I have a daughter but she's living all the way in Australia with her own children.'

Then Leslyn told Mr Martin all about the bonfire they were going to make.

'Do you have a guy as well?' he asked, his pale blue eyes suddenly coming alive. 'Do you know that they burn a guy on bonfire night?'

Leslyn hadn't really thought about a guy. Mr Martin had suddenly given her a good idea.

'I could give you an old jacket for the guy,' went on Mr Martin, 'if your mother don't mind, an old jacket for the guy.'

'She wouldn't mind, man,' cried Leslyn eagerly.

She watched Mr Martin as he walked slowly to his garden shed. A few moments later he was out again with an old brown striped jacket over his arm.

'Would you like some newspaper to burn as well?' he asked as he handed her the jacket over the fence.

'Yes,' said Leslyn at once, 'I'll come over and get them.'

And the next moment she was in Mr Martin's garden, fetching away a whole pile of old newspapers.

'Could I come to the fence and watch the

bonfire, do you think?' asked Mr Martin as she struggled away with the papers.

'You don't have to ask, man,' said Leslyn, turning back to look at him in surprise. 'You can watch,' she added, 'I'll come over and tell you when it's bonfire time.'

Leslyn dumped all the newspapers in their own garden shed then she skipped upstairs with the old brown jacket.

Both Nen and her mother were downstairs and in no time Leslyn made a very strange looking Guy Fawkes. She stuffed some of Nen's old dresses from the laundry basket into the brown jacket, then she pulled through some of the cloth as the head. She stuffed the head into a red woolly hat with a bob on top. Then she got a piece of cord and tied it around Guy Fawkes' waist.

But she hadn't stuffed the sleeves so they hung down limply.

'What's that you've got there?' Mars asked, when Leslyn came downstairs clutching her Guy Fawkes.

'Guy Fawkes,' said Leslyn, 'Ooooooh, I can hardly wait.'

'Where you got that old jacket from?' asked her mother.

'From Mr Martin next door,' said Leslyn, 'and he gave us a whole heap of newspapers as well for the bonfire.'

'You know I don't like you handling old things that I know nothing about,' said her mother, coming closer to have a look. 'And what you have stuffed up inside there,' she asked suspiciously.

'Only some of Nen's old dresses,' admitted Leslyn.

'Which old dresses?' asked Nen at once, coming out of the living room to have a look.

'Well I never!' she exclaimed, as she began to unstuff her dresses from Guy Fawkes, 'this little girl is a girl and a half, taking all my good-good clothes to say she stuffing Guy Fawkes.'

Leslyn sighed. At times she didn't know why grown-ups like to fret so much.

She had to stuff Guy Fawkes all over again, this time with old plastic bags and odds and ends that her mother got from the bottom of a cupboard.

But she wrung her hands in excitement when

she looked through the kitchen window and saw the dark garden outside . . . waiting.

And later that night, when they were all finished eating, Leslyn and her mother and father pulled on their coats and switched on the outside light at the back door. The whole back garden came softly into view.

Her father collected the other newspaper from the shed and down the garden path they all went, with Leslyn hopping ahead with her Guy Fawkes.

'Wait, wait, don't light it yet,' cried Leslyn suddenly as she remembered something.

Leslyn ran over to Mr Martin's quickly and banged on his door.

'Quick quick!' she said breathlessly, when he opened the door. 'Bonfire starting now.'

Then Leslyn ran back over again. She could feel her heart pounding with excitement.

Her mother and father had already dumped out all the bonfire papers and rags and things into the crate and were just waiting to scratch the match. Her father struck the first match to light the little twigs from underneath.

The little twigs caught afire but fizzled out after a while.

Her father lit them again and again. But each time they went out, much to Leslyn's impatience.

'Come on,' she shouted, dancing around the crate like a little witch. 'Come on.'

And the twigs seemed to have heard, for at

the very next match they stayed alight, and soon the newspapers and everything were crackling away.

They stood watching the flames licking the sides of the crate and growing bigger and brighter with each passing moment.

Soon it was roaring with flames, as the high heap of bonfire stuff was slowly eaten into.

Leslyn danced around it again, taking in the faces of Nen and Cousin Lucille and Cousin Frank at the upstairs bedroom window, and the small figure of Mr Martin leaning against his garden fence.

Then suddenly, in the midst of her dancing, Leslyn heard a big bang and saw something shooting up into the dark sky.

The next moment a shower of bright stars was bursting above her head.

It was so unexpected that Leslyn covered her face with her hands, hardly daring to look.

'It's fireworks,' cried Mars, 'it's coming from

the garden over there. Oh, look at that! Look Leslyn look!'

Leslyn took her hands from her face and looked just as a cluster of rockets went whizzing into the air. There were more bangs and flashes of gold and green and silver and red, dancing like rainbows above her head. Again and again the rockets went up exploding into showering fountains of colour around her.

'So that was fireworks,' Leslyn thought as she gazed up, star-struck by the beautiful sight. She had never seen anything before like it!

Their own bonfire was beginning to burn low now.

'You forgot to burn your Guy Fawkes, Leslyn,' said Mars suddenly as she glanced at Leslyn who was still clutching her Guy Fawkes.

But Leslyn hadn't forgotten.

'It's too late to burn him now,' she murmured dreamily.

CHAPTER 6

She Talks to Walls

'You must try and settle down to your work, Leslyn,' said Miss Sander, Leslyn's teacher. 'You can't keep getting up from your seat whenever you feel like it. You're distracting the others.'

Leslyn wasn't getting along so well at school. She got tired of sitting at her table for such long spells. She found the slightest excuse to get up.

She got up to borrow pencils and rubbers from the other children, even though she had her own in her pencil case. She got up to look at the pictures on the wall and to stare through the window pane.

She remembered how they used to have a lot of their lessons outside, back at her old school. There they would sit under the shade of a big shady tree in the grassy playground with the blue skies overhead.

Here she could hardly catch a glimpse of sky.

And her old teacher always wrote out their sums on the blackboard, then they did them in their exercise books. She didn't have to work in any Maths Book which was what Miss Sander had given her. The Maths Book made everything seem harder somehow.

Leslyn liked painting and reading. But she didn't like Maths.

She hadn't made any best friends as yet either.

At break time she played skipping and hopscotch with Josnara, the Indian girl from Bangladesh.

Sometimes she played with Lisa and Amanda and Jean, but Leslyn couldn't say that any one of them was her best friend. They all lived in the big block of Council flats on the estate behind the school, and they knew one another very well.

One afternoon Leslyn was very excited however. She had asked Lisa to come home and play with her and Lisa had asked her mum who said yes.

Mars was happy for Leslyn and she told Lisa's mother that they would walk her home when she was ready.

Leslyn's heart was glowing as Lisa walked home with them that afternoon. Maybe Lisa would even be her best friend.

She and Lisa had some bread with butter and jam then Leslyn took her up to her room and showed her all her toys. Her brown balata monkey which was made from a rubbery stuff that came from a special tree in Guyana, called Bullet-Wood tree. She showed her her small Amerindian girl chieftess doll with her beaded head-dress and she showed her her big stuffed puma which was a kind of mountain lion.

They made patterns on the carpet with Leslyn's sea shells which she kept in an old box, then they dressed up like market women. Leslyn showed Lisa how to wrap the cloth round and round her head so that it became a kind of flat pad to hold her basket.

'Let's look at television now,' said Lisa suddenly.

But Leslyn didn't want to look at television because it was so nice to have a friend for a change to play with.

'Man, let's play with Cheryl and Asana and Kwesi,' she said suddenly.

Lisa stared at her. She didn't know what on earth Leslyn was talking about.

'That's Cheryl over there,' said Leslyn pointing to the wall by her bed. 'That's Kwesi with the window, and that's Asana.' Cheryl and Asana and Kwesi were Leslyn's make-believe friends

and they played with her sometimes when she
was all alone.

'We could pretend we're going on a picnic,'
Leslyn went on, 'Asana, you bring the sand-
wiches,' she added, turning to the wall near the
door.

Just then Leslyn's mother called them down for
something to eat.

Mars had cooked peas and rice with salt-fish
cakes and stew to go with it. Leslyn looked at Lisa
anxiously, hoping that she would like it.

Lisa wrinkled up her nose a little at the strange
looking salt-fish cakes but she did eat some of the
food.

The next day at school, however, Lisa told the
other children all about Leslyn's home and the
food she ate, 'and she talks to walls,' she added
with a giggle.

'She's balmy,' sniggered Gary. 'Me dad says
they have to go back to their own country.'

'And why does she keep saying "Man" all the time,' joined in Amanda. 'Man, I don't like this. Man, I don't like that.' Everyone laughed.

Leslyn didn't say much as she walked home from school with her mother that afternoon. She felt too hurt inside. She couldn't explain it to Mars. She couldn't explain it to anyone.

But as soon as she got home she began to write a letter to her Grandma at the kitchen table.

Dear Grandma,

I hope you are well and you are fine. I am not so well becose I don't have anyone to play with and it is cold. You are luckey to be living in the sunshine. I miss you and my best friend Claire very much and my cosins very much. Please send me something for Christmas.

With love from your grandchile Leslyn

When Mars looked over her shoulder and saw the letter she told Leslyn how to spell 'because' and 'lucky' and 'cousins' and 'grandchild' correctly, and then she added, 'You don't want your Grandma to feel that you're unhappy. You know how she likes to worry.'

'Yes,' said Leslyn, in a bleaky kind of voice, 'but I don't have anyone to play with and the children at school don't even like me. Nobody likes me. Peter Brooms keep calling me gollywog and chocolate face. Gary Mulking keep saying that we have to go back to our own country. Why we had to come to this country anyway?' she finished off.

'You know we came here to be with Daddy,' said her mother coming around to give her a hug. 'Don't worry with those stupid boys at school,' she went on. 'You'll make friends, but it takes time. You haven't even been going to school for a good three weeks as yet.'

But it's time enough for me, thought Leslyn as she curled herself on the carpet in front of the television. At least the television was a kind of friend.

CHAPTER 7

It's the Frog

Saturday morning, and Leslyn kept getting into everyone's way because everyone was at home – Cousin Lucille, Cousin Frank, her father.

Mars, who wasn't accustomed to spending so much time cooped up indoors, was feeling a bit down. 'I don't think I can survive in this place,' she said, pulling her dressing gown closer around her, 'I'm a sun-woman.'

'Tell you what,' said Leslyn's father suddenly. 'Let's get dressed quickly and I'll take you down to Shepherd's Bush Market to get a little West Indian atmosphere. You can get some things for your hair,' he went on, trying to cheer Mars up, 'and afterwards we can jump on a bus to one of the shopping centres.'

'It's so cold,' murmured Mars. She didn't enjoy walking about in the cold, but anything was better than spending the entire Saturday at home.

So in about an hour's time Leslyn and her mother and father were walking down the pavement, past the closed-up houses on their street, and out on to the busy main road where streams of traffic went by.

Soon they were at the Underground station with its ticket machines and people hurrying in all directions to catch trains.

Leslyn, who had never been on the Underground before, gasped when they came to the long shiny moving escalators.

She gripped her father's hand tightly as they went down.

She thought the escalators were like moving slides with steps on them, as she watched the heads of the people going up on the other side – moving slides going up and down in the earth.

She was so busy watching the other side that she almost tripped when they got to the bottom of theirs, even though she was holding her father's hand.

Then they had to find their way. After walking through a long tunnel and up and down stairs, they finally came to a crowded platform.

Leslyn's father went up to look at the big Underground map that was stuck up against the wall. It looked very confusing to Leslyn.

'I think we can take the Circle Line and change at Notting Hill Gate,' her father was saying, as he tried to work things out. They were going to Shepherd's Bush Market first.

Just then the big silver grey train was rumbling through the dark hole of the tunnel and pulling up alongside their platform.

'Which train is this? Which train is this?' asked Leslyn's father, looking around him quickly.

'It's the Circle Line,' said a tall man with a briefcase.

'Quick,' said Leslyn's father, grabbing hold of her hand, 'quick, this is our train,' and he pushed his way through on to the train.

Mars, who was a bit confused, dashed into the carriage that was nearest to her.

'Mars, Mars!' screamed Leslyn. She didn't want her mother to be separated from them.

But the train doors were already closing.

'Mars! Mars!' screamed Leslyn again, shaking her father's arm. Some of the people on the train stared as her father tried to quieten her down.

'It's all right,' he was saying, 'she's only in the next carriage. We'll get off at the next stop and go across with her.'

What if her mother got lost among all those people? Leslyn was thinking. What if they never saw her again? And it was frightening the way the big train doors suddenly seemed to snap shut by themselves.

Mars wasn't lost however. At the very next stop they hurried across into the next carriage, and there she was safe and sound.

But Leslyn was glad when they were up in the open streets again.

'Oh Boy!' she breathed in relief.

At Shepherd's Bush Market calypso music was playing in the background and Mars began to shake-up her waist a little as she moved around, stopping here and there to pick up some nice things for her skin and hair.

Leslyn felt good to see her mother looking cheerful again.

The market reminded Leslyn of home. She could see mangoes, even though they were a bit wrinkled, and she could see dried coconuts, plantains and sugarcane.

They bought some plantains and saltfish which her father loved and they bought a red, gold and green Rasta beret for Leslyn, who put it on her head right away, pulling it down over her ears to get them warm.

'Peace and love,' said the Rasta man selling the berets as they left the market.

Leslyn and her mother and father had some fish and chips to eat at a nearby restaurant. Then they hopped on to a red double decker bus across the street.

Leslyn managed to get a seat by the window upstairs. She could see all that was going on outside.

The signs of Christmas were everywhere, as it was already the end of November.

She stared down at the pavements which seemed to be packed with moving people. People were pouring in and out of stores. She could see the store windows decorated with frost and dressed-up huge Christmas trees. She could see brightly wrapped presents and a giant-sized poster of Santa Claus with his sleigh on one high

building. She could see signs saying 'Merry Christmas'.

It was like being in a different world, Leslyn thought when they came off the bus and began to move around. She stared up at the sea of faces going by all around her.

'Hold my hand,' her mother warned. 'This isn't like Guyana. You can't afford to get lost.'

Leslyn didn't like shopping but this particular afternoon she didn't mind. Most of the stores they went into were nice and warm with soft carpets and lots of different things to see.

While her mother and father were busy shopping around she found plenty to occupy her.

At one big department store Christmas carols were being played softly in the background. While her mother and father were deciding whether they could afford to buy her a new anorak, she slipped back down on the escalator to the Toy Section which she had noticed while going up.

Leslyn had never seen so many toys in all her life. She didn't know where to start looking. As she went along she looked at teddybears and dolls and games and balls. She pulled the trigger of small space guns. She looked at books and paints. Other children were looking around too.

Then in the far corner of a shelf at the back something caught Leslyn's eye.

It was a big green frog, with saddish looking black eyes, sitting on a box. The frog had a red key

sticking in its back and it was the only one of its kind sitting beside the other smaller toys.

Leslyn was drawn to the frog and she couldn't help wondering what the key was for.

A few moments later she was reaching up for the frog on the box. A few moments later she had taken the frog from the box and was winding the little key in its back, round and round and round, until it could go no further.

Then she placed it back on the shelf.

She expected the frog to do something. But she didn't know it was going to behave like that.

The next moment the big green frog was hopping violently around, with a clanking sound, knocking most of the smaller toys around it, out of its way.

Little plastic games and cars and rubber balls were flying through the air and scattering all around on the carpet below, while the frog hopped away merrily.

Then before Leslyn could stop it, the big green frog took a clean leap and landed on the floor just by her feet. Two of the salesgirls from around the counter came hurrying to see what the noise was all about. Some of the other customers were also looking.

Leslyn felt a bit afraid because with that last leap the big green frog had stopped hopping completely.

Leslyn bent hurriedly and began helping to pick up the scattered toys from around the floor.

One of the salesgirls picked up the frog and began winding it again, while the other one said in a scolding kind of voice, 'You aren't allowed to take toys from the display.'

'Looks as if it's all right,' said the salesgirl who had been winding the frog.

To Leslyn's relief when she rested it down on the floor it began to hop madly around again.

And just then her mother and father who had been looking all around for her came along.

'What's the matter?' asked Mars who sensed that something had just happened. 'Why can't you keep with us?'

The salesgirl replaced the frog on the shelf and

Leslyn began to walk away with her mother and father.

'It's the frog,' she said staring back over her shoulder at the big green frog which was sitting neatly on its box again. She was almost certain that this time the frog's sad black eyes were smiling.

CHAPTER 8

A Real Snowman

About a week before Christmas it began to snow, lightly at first, then more and more thickly.

Leslyn, who was at home for the Christmas holidays, didn't know it was snowing until she came downstairs. Then she saw the white swirling down through a gap in the window curtains.

She rushed to the window and gasped at the sight outside.

Everywhere was white.

The roofs of the brown brick houses across the street and the chimneys, the gardens, the fence and even the cars, parked a little way up the street, were all white.

She had heard about snow. She had seen it in books, and on television since coming over. But she had never seen it for real.

'It's snowing! It's snowing, Mars, it's snowing,' she sang, twirling around at the window.

Her mother, who had just come downstairs, came running to the window too and they both stood watching the falling snow, like thousands and thousands of tiny white wings flurrying down from heaven.

'I want to go outside and catch some,' cried Leslyn excitedly. 'I want to go out and catch some,' and the next thing she was dashing to the door.

'You're crazy little girl?' called out Mars behind her, 'you can't go outside in your nightgown.'

Leslyn pulled on her coat over her nightgown then she sat at the bottom of the steps and pulled on her short boots.

'Wait for me,' cried Mars suddenly as Leslyn was about to open the door and Leslyn watched her mother slipping into her father's old anorak then they both stepped outside.

The snow swirled in their faces.

Leslyn held out her hands and spun around trying to catch some snowflakes but as soon as they touched her warm palm they melted. They melted on her tongue too but some gathered on the hood and sleeves of her coat and all over her mother's anorak. Leslyn and her mother crunched around in the snow for a while.

And for the rest of that day it went on snowing. Every time Leslyn looked outside it seemed as if the white snow blanket in the front garden had risen a little higher.

'I can't stand all this snow,' grumbled Nen who had come downstairs. 'I suppose it will make some people happy though. They always talk about white Christmas. Give me my sunshine any day,' she added.

At times Leslyn felt sorry for Nen who was always complaining about how the cold made her bones ache.

'Why don't you go back home then, to live?' she asked Nen.

But Nen didn't seem to hear her.

'It's terrible when it freezes and becomes all icy,' she went on, 'then when it melts, that is another story, all brown and slushy. You can't even say you're going for a walk.'

'Go back to Guyana and live then,' said Leslyn again, 'in the sunshine.'

'Go back to Guyana,' said Nen, her eyes looking wistful. 'I don't have anyone to go back to in Guyana. All my children live in this country.' But Nen sounded very much as if she would prefer to spend her old age in the sunshine than in the cold.

'You could go for a holiday,' suggested Leslyn, 'to see your friends. My Grandma is coming to see us next year for a holiday so you could go back home for a holiday too. That would be fair.' And she drew a nice picture with a big red sun to cheer Nen up.

It had stopped snowing by this time and when Leslyn looked outside again she saw the snow lying white and thick and crisp and powdery in the garden.

Then she had a lovely idea. As lovely as a rainbow in a dark grey sky.

She had seen some children doing the very thing on television a few days ago.

Leslyn didn't tell anyone what it was she was going to do but she slipped into the kitchen and got her mother's rubber gloves, then she slipped out quietly into the front garden.

She pulled on the pink gloves quickly then she stooped down in the middle of the garden and began to gather up snow for all she was worth, scraping it together in a heap.

Yes, she was going to make a snowman. A real snowman. That was the very thing she was going to make and give her mother and everyone else a good surprise.

Leslyn worked fast as already she could feel the cold biting through the thin rubber she was wearing. But she went on working, scraping the snow and smoothing it around the heap in the middle.

Although her poor fingers were burning she didn't stop as her heart was into making the snowman. Her fingers began to feel numb and stiff. They were stinging like anything. Still Leslyn persevered.

Then she could stand it no longer. Gathering up the last handful of snow she slapped it on top, as the head of the snowman and she dashed into the house, the tears streaming down her cheeks.

'Owh, Owh, my hands,' she moaned, pulling off the gloves.

Her fingers were stiff and red and very painful.

'Look at your hands!' exclaimed Mars when she saw Leslyn's fingers. 'Oh Leslyn, what have you been doing?'

'Making a snowman,' said Leslyn, still crying.

Mars took Leslyn's hand within her own and began to massage her fingers gently but that only seemed to make them hurt all the more and Leslyn cried out louder.

'Go and sit by the heater in the living room,' said Mars, 'and I'll bring some hot blackcurrant drink for you.'

Leslyn went into the living room and curled herself before the heater and little by little her fingers began to feel less and less stiff.

'You've still managed to make a nice little snowman,' said her mother comfortingly, when she had come back into the room with the blackcurrant. She had stood for a moment at the window, looking at the small imperfect snowman in the middle of the garden.

'She means to get every ounce of value outa this life,' said Nen, glancing across to where Leslyn sat.

And as Leslyn sat drinking her drink and feeling better she couldn't help thinking that even though there was something cold and stingy about winter outside, there was also something warm and cosy and inside about it too.

CHAPTER 9

It's From Grandma!

By Christmas Eve day the house was smelling nice and Christmassy, Leslyn thought.

Her mother had made a big black fruit cake and a special Guyanese dish called pepperpot. Leslyn loved to see her mother pouring in the thick dark spicy cassareep into the pot with the different meats, and to hear it bubbling up.

She had helped her father to decorate the Christmas tree, and there it stood, in a corner of the living room, looking like Christmas itself — with its bright decorations and snowy angel hair and little Father Christmas chocolates which she was very tempted to start eating.

She had already hung up a big pillow case on the hook behind her bedroom door for her presents, because she was hoping to get a lot of them.

She had already run round to Mr Martin's and slipped a Christmas card for him through his door. They had been thinking of inviting Mr Martin over to lunch on Christmas Day, but Mr Martin was already invited by the people who lived a few doors away.

The only thing that made Leslyn feel a bit sad

in the midst of all the Christmas cheer was that they hadn't heard from grandma. She had been hoping all week that the postman would bring something from her, even if it was only a Christmas card. She had already sent her grandma a Christmas card with lots of kisses inside.

She kept seeing her grandma's face as she stared outside at the little snowman who was standing exactly as she'd left him in the snow covered garden. She remembered how she and her grandma used to like going to the seawalls back home. Her grandma would sit on a bench with the Atlantic breeze playing on her face. And she, Leslyn, would run around on the beach below with the other children.

In the midst of her thoughts about back home Leslyn's heart skipped a beat, because the postman was coming along the pavement with his brown sack. Maybe this time he would bring something from grandma.

The postman, who was making his second round for the morning, kept going into all the gates along the pavement. But to Leslyn's disappointment he went straight by theirs.

The rest of Christmas Eve went by quickly after that.

Leslyn had to pop out to the supermarket with her father to get a few last minute things and soon they were at the table having dinner.

Leslyn had just started eating when the door bell rang.

'I'll get it,' she said, jumping up at once.

'Ask who it is first, before opening the door,' called out Mars behind her.

'Who's it?' Leslyn called, her hand waiting impatiently to turn the door knob.

'Carol singers,' came the answer from muffled voices.

Leslyn opened the door quickly, and who should be standing there but Lisa Jones and Sharon Parker, who were in her class and two other children who lived up on the housing estate.

Before Leslyn could recover from her shock, they all broke into singing, 'Good King Wincelaust'.

Mars got up from the table to get them some money, and as soon as they got it, they finished off singing hurriedly.

'Merry Christmas, Leslyn,' called out Lisa, as they made their way to the gate.

'Merry Christmas' called back Leslyn, staring after them longingly. She would have loved to have gone carol singing with them but nobody had asked her.

After dinner Leslyn was sitting in the living room with everyone else watching a comedy programme on TV Leslyn thought how nice everything looked. The programme was funny but she still kept flashing back to her grandma.

Suddenly the doorbell rang again.

Leslyn dashed outside to answer it at once. Mars got up and came behind her.

Leslyn forgot to ask, 'Who is it?' this time and opened the door.

The small figure of Mr Martin was standing there, bundled up in his grey coat, and clutching a few parcels in his hand.

'Come on in,' said Mars inviting him in from the cold.

Mr Martin came in.

'Would these be for you?' he asked in his trembly voice holding out a letter and a flattish brown parcel to Mars. 'The postman left them today but they don't belong to me. Allenye, it says.'

'That's us! That's us!' cried Leslyn excitedly.

'Why, it's from Grandma,' Mars was exclaiming in surprise, 'the letter's for me and the parcel is for you, Leslyn.'

'For me,' shrieked Leslyn, 'from Grandma?'

Leslyn couldn't believe it. She grabbed hold of the parcel and went running into the kitchen and back out into the hall and into the living room clutching the parcel and shrieking, 'It's from Grandma! It's from Grandma!'

'Calm yourself child,' said Nen as an excited Leslyn almost fell into her lap.

But Leslyn only planted a kiss on her cheek and went on chanting 'It's from Grandma. It's from Grandma.'

'We might as well take off the television until the confusion finishes,' said Cousin Frank a little peevishly, and turning to Leslyn's father he said,

'you can invite Mr Martin in for a drink.'

Mr Martin didn't want anything strong to drink so Mars gave him a glass of ginger beer and a slice of her Christmas cake, even though it wasn't Christmas Day as yet.

Mr Martin had something else in a plastic bag with him and when he was leaving he took it out and gave it to Leslyn.

'This is from me,' he said, handing Leslyn a nicely wrapped up small present.

Leslyn thanked him with a glowing face. With the present from her grandma, everything seemed just right for Christmas now.

Christmas morning came quickly because Leslyn woke up early. It was still dark so she switched on the light above her head.

Immediately her eyes went to the bulging pillow case behind the door. She had decided to leave her grandma's present for last.

With tingling fingers Leslyn took down the pillow case from behind the door. Already she could see the head of a brownish, orange teddy

bear sticking out from the top, which was one of the things she really wanted.

Leslyn took out the teddybear which had a red bow around its neck, and gave it a big squeeze, then she emptied the other things out on to her bed. There was a painting set and drawing book and a ball with two rackets. Then she opened Mr Martin's present which was a box of peppermints.

Then it was time for her grandma's present.

Leslyn sat on the edge of her bed and began to undo the flattish brown parcel. How she loved undoing parcels. She pulled away the tape that was running all around the parcel. She pulled away the brown paper. Then another sheet of brown paper. Then another sheet of brown paper. Her grandma didn't make fun when she was posting parcels. She could feel the excitement rising within her.

At last Leslyn pulled away all of the paper. And what do you think was folded up neatly before her? Leslyn's eyes shone as she stared – it was a red masquerade suit, a real masquerade suit, with a small bamboo flute to go with it.

Her grandma had remembered how much she liked to watch the masquerade dancers at Christmas time. Leslyn would always dash outside on to the pavement back home, whenever she heard the slightest sound of a drum or flute playing.

She would know it was the masquerade men coming and so would everyone who lived nearby.

In no time the pavement would be full of people and Leslyn would be jumping up and down in the air as the music got louder and louder and the band came closer and closer. Then people would throw money on to the street as the dancing men came by in their bright glistening costumes and the men would dance right down to the ground and pick up the coins.

Leslyn loved seeing that and loved seeing the stilt-man who was always just behind the band high high up on his stilts.

Grandma had remembered all that, and had made Leslyn's masquerade suit exactly how the men in Guyana wore them – the tight-fitting red velvet top had beads and sequins all over. And so did the short, flouncy, red velvet skirt.

Leslyn couldn't wait to try on the suit and give her mother and father a surprise.

She was just pulling off her nightie when she noticed something else, lying among the brown paper.

It was a small white envelope and Leslyn reached for it at once, wondering what was inside.

The envelope wasn't sealed and she quickly opened it and pulled out a folded up note, which felt as if it had some little thing inside.

Heart beating fast, Leslyn opened out the note and then the piece of tissue that was inside. A small black flattish shiny seed stared up at her from the white paper.

At first Leslyn didn't recognise what it was. Then she did.

It was a tamarind seed. The seed from a ripe tamarind. The seed that was supposed to bring luck!

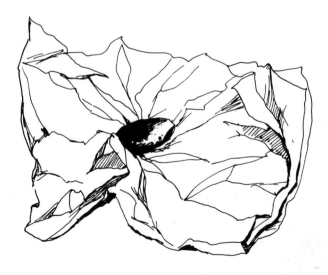

Leslyn could only stare at it in wonder.

She read the note that her grandma had sent along with the seed. It said:

Dear Leslyn,

Keep this tamarind seed for luck. I hope that it brings you a lot of luck and happiness.

Leslyn folded up her lucky tamarind seed carefully. Just imagine her grandma thinking of sending her that. It was a really special Christmas gift.

Leslyn was so happy that she pulled on her red masquerade suit, and began blowing her flute and flouncing all around her bedroom, like the masquerade men did.

Of course the flute music woke up the whole household but as Leslyn danced away all her thoughts were fixed on the future luck that her tamarind seed was going to bring her.

CHAPTER 10

Thanks for Making Me Lucky, and Famous Too

January was a cold dark month.

Leslyn was back at school again and nothing very lucky had happened to her so far. But she never doubted for a moment that it would.

She still had her lucky tamarind seed wrapped up in the bit of tissue paper at the bottom of her drawer. She hadn't taken it to school to show any of the children because she was afraid of losing it.

But she spoke about it a lot.

Whenever she did her eyes became all shiny and excited.

'My grandma says it's going to bring me luck,' she kept saying happily. 'It's a lucky seed.'

'Bet it's just a silly old seed and not a lucky one,' said Gary, his voice sounding jealous.

'She's lying,' laughed Mick.

'Bet she doesn't even have a seed,' said Jonathan.

Some of the children believed her though and Leslyn took it to school to show them.

'Just a silly seed,' said Gary, pretending that he

wasn't interested as Leslyn slowly undid the piece of tissue that her seed was wrapped in.

The children who had crowded around her drew their breath when the small black flattish seed was lying before them.

None of them had ever seen a seed exactly like that one before. It did look strange lying there against the white tissue. It did look a little magic looking. The kind of seed that could bring luck.

Even Gary wouldn't help leaning across the table to have a look, though he was still muttering, 'just a silly seed.'

After showing the children, Leslyn put away her lucky seed again.

January slipped by into February.

Still nothing that was specially lucky happened to her and she began to get a bit impatient.

'Couldn't I get a brown dog then?' she asked her mother one afternoon, after looking at a programme on telly about a big brown dog. It had suddenly dawned upon her that a dog could be the answer to all her problems.

A clever brown dog just like the one she'd seen. A dog that could fetch newspapers and letters and do tricks and save babies from drowning and people from being kidnapped. A dog that she could love and take for walks. A dog that would never make her feel lonely again.

But her mother wouldn't even take her seriously.

'You think you can keep a dog just like that?' she said lightly, looking up from the letter she was writing. 'You have to have somewhere to put a dog. You have to look after it. Take it for walks.'

'I know. I know,' said Leslyn impatiently.

She knew she wasn't going to get a big brown dog. Just by looking at her mother's face she could tell.

February slipped into March.

Leslyn couldn't hide her disappointment that she hadn't made a best friend as yet. Mars allowed her to play down at the park with the other children as the afternoons were getting bright again. Leslyn couldn't say that anyone was her best friend though. They played with her but they all had their special friends.

One morning Leslyn woke up to find some yellow daffodils nodding their heads in the front garden. To her surprise when she had a good look, she could see other little flowers coming out, not only in their garden, but in all the gardens along her street.

She began to notice that more people were coming outdoors too. Some of the women across the street came out to clean their windows. Mr Martin had started to potter around his garden more. Even Nen opened her bedroom window and stood sniffing the fresh air, as she remarked, 'Spring is definitely here.'

In spite of herself Leslyn began to feel a funny

feeling inside her. A nice funny feeling as if everything was suddenly coming alive around her.

And one soft Spring morning, just as her teacher
was about to mark names, the classroom door was
pushed open and in walked the headmistress with
a new girl behind her.

The whole class perked up as the headmistress
said, 'This is Imogen, Miss Sander, whom I was
telling you about.'

Gary and Jonathan exchanged sniggering
glances as if they thought the name funny.

Leslyn stared at Imogen whose eyes caught
hers for a moment. Leslyn began to feel excited.
Imogen had the kind of look . . . Leslyn didn't
know how to explain it. The kind of look that was
full of secrets and surprises. As if anything could
happen when she was around. She also looked a
bit frightened too.

As soon as the headmistress had left, Leslyn got
up quickly from her seat and went across to the
teacher's table.

'Please Miss, she can sit at my table,' she said
quietly, hoping desperately that her teacher
would say yes.

Miss Sander glanced around the classroom.
There was an empty chair at Leslyn's table, and
there was no harm.

'All right,' she said. 'You're very kind, Leslyn.
You can show Imogen where everything is for
today.'

For the rest of that day Leslyn took Imogen under her wing. She showed her the Girls' Cloakroom and toilets. She took her to measure her height against the 'How Tall Are You?' sign.

At break time they played together on the climbing frame, hanging upside down and facing each other.

Imogen was from Birmingham and spoke in a low sing-song voice, her black hair tumbling wildly around her face, like a little gypsy.

That afternoon when school was over they walked along the pavement together, until they got to the part where Imogen and her mother had to turn off. Mars and Imogen's mother had been laughing and talking as they walked ahead a bit. Leslyn felt good inside. Imogen's mother was called Zoe and her hair was as black and wild looking as Imogen's.

The very next afternoon Zoe invited Leslyn and Mars home for a cup of tea. To Leslyn's surprise Imogen and her mother lived in one of the houses in the side street, not too far from their own home. She wouldn't have to cross the busy mainroad if she wanted to come and see Imogen. Leslyn couldn't believe her luck.

While Zoe was making the tea and chatting with her mother downstairs, she and Imogen were running around upstairs in Imogen's room. They played on her drumset. Imogen showed Leslyn her box of postcards which she'd been collecting and she gave Leslyn a nice one with a blue sea and sandy beach. Leslyn couldn't tell the last time she had so much fun.

As the days got warmer and warmer Leslyn and Imogen became best friends.

Imogen was always finding some little thing. She was the one who discovered the grey nest in the big tree right at the back of the school yard. The nest was half-hidden among the leaves, but Imogen had spotted it and took Leslyn to see it, and to see the black bird that kept flying in and out of it.

'Gosh!' Leslyn had cried out in wonder.

Sometimes when Imogen's mother wanted to go out she would bring Imogen across to stay. Imogen's mother and father were divorced. And sometimes when Mars had to go out she would take Leslyn across. Mars had found a drama group to join and these days she seemed more like the bouncy old Mars that Leslyn knew.

One Saturday afternoon there was a fair at the nearby community centre and Leslyn and Imogen were there.

The fair was being held on the open grounds and both Mars and Zoe were helping out at one of the stalls. There were lots of stalls selling cakes and drinks and books and things. There was a magician and people telling stories in one corner of the ground. There were inflatables and a tent where children kept going to get their faces painted.

Imogen wanted her face painted to look like Dracula and Leslyn wanted to look like a clown.

When they were finished they began chasing each other round and round. A photographer who was taking pictures asked if he could take theirs. So Leslyn and Imogen posed for him. He asked them their names too, but in a little while they had forgotten all about him.

But a few afternoons later Leslyn's father came in with a newspaper.

'Anybody know these two children here?' he asked in a casual voice.

'Which children?' asked Leslyn, leaping up from the table.

Her father held open the papers for her and

Leslyn gasped. Right there in the middle of the page was a picture of herself and Imogen in painted faces.

'Man! We're famous,' she cried.

'I suppose so,' said her father laughing.

Mars and Nen had a look at the picture which had Leslyn's and Imogen's names below and a little write up about the fair.

'Trust them to get their pictures in the papers,' murmured Nen.

'Could I take it across and show Imogen?' asked Leslyn excitedly.

'All right,' said her mother, 'walk carefully.'

But before Leslyn left with the newspaper she suddenly dashed upstairs and took out her tamarind seed that her grandma had sent her.

She held the seed in the palm of her hand and whispered, 'Thanks for making me lucky, and famous too.'